Straight Up From the Teacup

Toni Dupree

STRAIGHT UP FROM THE TEACUP

Toni Dupree

Cover Design By:
Sayla, LLC
http://sayla.io
contact@sayla.io

Pearly Gates Publishing LLC
INSPIRING CHRISTIAN AUTHORS TO BE AUTHORS
Pearly Gates Publishing, LLC, Houston, Texas

Straight Up From the Teacup

Straight Up From the Teacup

Copyright © 2018
Toni Dupree

All Rights Reserved.
No portion of this publication may be reproduced, stored in any electronic system, or transmitted in any form or by any means (electronic, mechanical, photocopy, recording, or otherwise) without written permission from the author or publisher. Brief quotations may be used in literary reviews.

ISBN 13: 978-1-947445-21-5
Library of Congress Control Number: 2018941393

For information and bulk ordering, contact:
Pearly Gates Publishing, LLC
Angela Edwards, CEO
P.O. Box 62287
Houston, TX 77205
BestSeller@PearlyGatesPublishing.com

DEDICATION

To my Mom: Happy Birthday, JT!
Thank you for pouring real life lessons into me.
These lessons will continue to sculpt my life
and the lives of the people I touch.

I love you.

Forever, always, and just because…

ACKNOWLEDGEMENTS

To my Love, Mr. Richard McFarland: Thank you for your unending encouragement and support!

To Mrs. Toni Reed: You give me nothing but the realest, most raw, unadulterated life in every conversation. Thank you!

Mrs. Angela Edwards, my Publisher: You are the absolute best! Thank you for the peaceful pushes at just the right times during this project that have allowed me to challenge myself. It looks like we are a great team!

Ms. Rosalyn Grizzard, my Tea Guru: Thank you so much for being a great resource!

Mrs. Blessing Osakue, my Most Talented Photographer and Creative Designer: Thank you for sharing your beautiful gift with me. I knew when we met that we would create beautiful work together—and we are doing just that!

To the host of Friends, Collaborators, and Colleagues who inspire and support me: Thank you as well!

"Whenever you think you don't have the right words to say, say them anyway. Only a misguided heart can render the wrong words."
~ **Toni Dupree** ~

PREFACE

When I was growing up, I always hated the hypocrisy and mediocrity of the important people around me. You see, they always spoke broad and bold; however, when faced with a situation that required them to show up, they couldn't or wouldn't. This taught me to pay closer attention to what's done and less to what's said.

I started asking myself particular questions geared to specific situations like:

"Can I be resourceful in this situation?"

"Can I be myself?"

"Is this a likeable situation or is it for pretense?"

These questions became more and more relevant as an adult. I started thinking about why I engage in relationships where I always have to tell grown people something about themselves or about the way they are treating me. I **HATE** having to tell adults something about their behavior. It's the worst! They always give you that, *"Who the* **HELL** *are YOU to be telling me anything?"* attitude. **UGH! I HATE IT!** But what's the alternative? Grabbing the jar of Vaseline, greasing up my face with it, removing the earrings, and going blow-for-blow? *I don't think so!*

I'm the type of person who likes to share and offer something to make any situation better…not bitter. It's important to know the good that you come with. Even if you don't like me, it's not because I dimmed your light. I'm from the south, damnit! We finesse our situations using lady-like assertiveness. So, I make conscious decisions to bow out gracefully from any situations projected on to me that attempt to make me the scapegoat or casualty of other people's bad decisions. It's very important to know: Why do we choose to do the things we do? The best way to answer that question is to get real with yourself.

THAT, my friends, is your *REAL* tea!

"Read and allow your mind to take you on an amazing journey where only your imagination can travel."
~ Toni Dupree ~

Tea is a wonderful beverage that warms the soul with a host of healthy benefits, all while being enjoyed by the tea-lover.

People drink tea for many different reasons:

- ❖ It has calming properties.
- ❖ It has healing properties.
- ❖ It's trendy.
- ❖ It tastes delicious.
- ❖ It's more calming than a cup of coffee.
- ❖ It's a stress-reliever.

"Improving Me Adds Value To the Way I See You."
~ Toni Dupree ~

Tea is a lot like a good, ole visit with a great friend. If I'm having company, I may serve Lemon Ginger, Hibiscus, or Earl Grey Tea—mainly because they are just a few of my personal favorites. Those particular teas are pretty easy to flavor to one's liking.

When I'm talking to people, sometimes I'm thinking about what type of tea we would drink to hash out the conversation. Other times I might consider what 'tea name' I would give the conversation. For example, if I wanted to discuss weight with someone, I would serve Parsley Tea because I would want to set a stage for the mood of a healthy chat. See, back in the day, my grandmother would serve tea to her guests after dinner. Tea helped with digestion, as well as made the visit relaxing and peaceful.

I want this book to have that same type of feel. Let's work together to set the stage for the outcome we want to achieve from our social interactions by relating them to tea!

Of course, if we are on the phone, we can't physically serve tea but what we can do is make the person on the other end a participant in the conversation…not our audience. They didn't call to hear you lecture. A conversation takes two. Always be mindful of your tone during a call. For example, if there is bad blood between the two of you, address it first. Remember, though: Do not bring a problem with a solution. There's a lot to be said for addressing the elephant "in the room". Acknowledge there's an issue but make a point to preserve the relationship. Try stating something like, "I understand things haven't been the greatest between us, but I wanted to let you know I was thinking of you."

That's an example of sipping "Soothing Tea"!

Table of Contents

DEDICATION	VI
ACKNOWLEDGEMENTS	VII
PREFACE	IX
THE TEA	XIII
POURING THE TEA	1
EGYPTIAN LICORICE TEA	7
THE RASPBERRY TEA BIT	11
LET'S CHAI TEA AND TALK	27
EARL GREY STYLE	39
SALTED CARAMEL	45
DETOXIFY WITH TEA	52
FINESSING THE TEA BAG	56

THE STEEP	60
TALK ABOUT YOUR TEAS	64
ABOUT THE AUTHOR	72
CONNECT WITH TONI DUPREE	76
OTHER PUBLICATIONS BY & WITH TONI DUPREE	77
TONI'S QUOTES – "TELL IT LIKE IT IS TEAS!"	79

Share your conversation like the pour of a hot, friendly cup of tea.

Twenty or more years ago, it was a special honor to be asked to pour tea. It would have made the social column of the local paper. The tea-pourer is the guardian of the pot, which implies perfect social graces.

Today, pouring someone's tea isn't recognized as newsworthy but can still be seen as invasive and a bit gossipy. There are other times we find a pouring of another's tea pretty entertaining. It's all about timing, place, and content, correct? There's actually a whole revenue stream to support this ideology. So, why wouldn't it be socially-acceptable?

This is where being socially-conscious comes into play.

I recall a time when I poured someone's tea when I was a child. My favorite aunt's husband (who is now deceased) was particularly "friendly" with one of my mother's girlfriends (I know this because I was eaves-dropping at my mom's bedroom door). Well, I felt that someone had to put a stop to the wrongdoing.

My grandmother was my buddy, baby! We saw each other quite often (being an only child, that was my norm). Well, when I went over to my grandparents' house that weekend, I shared what I had overheard my mother saying.

Slight pause here: The unfortunate thing about pouring someone else's tea is the amount of harm it does to others.

My grandmother was very loyal to me but the information I poured was severe. In that moment, it didn't matter that we were buddies because this involved her daughter. As such, she had to do something about this newfound knowledge. My grandmother's decision to do something involved my mother, her girlfriend, my aunt, and her husband.

My need to pour this tea to my grandmother affected all of those relationships in a negative way. My being a child, I didn't understand the magnitude of my choice…until my mother got a hold of me. I'm grown now, but I will never forget that dreadful pouring incident. It doesn't matter that I didn't mean to hurt all of those people; I did, and my mother had to take responsibility for my actions. I vowed to never make anyone else responsible for my actions again.

You, my friend, are not TMZ TV. "He's a lawyer." LOL! The interesting thing about choosing to pour another's tea is that it's not your story to tell! You might as well shout to the world, "I HAVE ABSOLUTELY NOTHING GOING ON IN MY LIFE, SO I'M GOING TO TALK ABOUT YOU!" What that behavior really says is the person sharing isn't comfortable with their own personal "stuff" to share.

Now, there is always another way to view things. People talk about a HOT topic! On the other end are those people who pour another's tea only if they have been wronged (that way, it's justifiable). Look: This is not about being some type of goodie-two-shoes. It's about being cognizant of your behavior and how that behavior impacts another person. It's also important to know if what you are sharing is shareable information.

Toni Dupree

Grace + Civility = Magic
~ Toni Dupree ~

The sharp bite of reality.

I attribute the way I am to the fact that my mom made it a point to let me know:

"My S**t Stank."

Knowing that my s**t stank is an important factor in not taking myself too seriously. Although we all know everything isn't about us, in this world of confusion and offbeat power, it's easy to get it twisted.

Fortunately for me, JT made it a point to let me know she was my only fan who would be on my bandwagon. This helped me understand the "peoply stuff". In its simplest terms, "peoply stuff" is the nonsense that has absolutely nothing to do with me.

The benefit of knowing your s**t stanks gives you the firsthand ability to deal with your own nonsense and not project it onto another by making them your scapegoat just because you don't want to deal with your own s**t!

If I manage "me", you won't have to!

"The gift of laughter is wonderful. The ability to laugh at yourself offers a special kind of freedom."
~ **Toni Dupree** ~

The tart with a hint of sweetness that speaks to the soul.

Raspberry Tea is sweet but remember: It has a zing of tartness. That "tartness" is the truth. Make certain when you decide to pour that you understand and have considered every outcome. We all know the truth can stand on its own but the question is: Can you?

A few of my punches to the gut have been because I didn't understand that when the truth is poured, the focus is on who's pouring. Let me explain, as it can get very tricky.

People will already know what you are saying to them is true but still choose to respond ridiculously because it's YOU who's doing the pouring. This is why I believe it's a must that you understand that your pour can go either way. So, ask yourself these questions:

❖ Why are you pouring their tea (in other words, why are YOU telling them this information)?

- ❖ Is this pour (the truth) for you or them?
- ❖ Will they be better for knowing or not knowing?

It's very possible you could lose a friend or acquaintance because you were the wrong person to pour. If you're okay with that possibility, then pour on.

The Clique

Growing up as an only child, I always longed to be a part of a 'clique' — you know…that slick group of ladies who were "fly as hell" and could stop traffic (too many movies, I guess). LOL! As an adult, I still wanted to be affiliated with that same type of lady but there are factors to be considered such as:

- ❖ Insecurities.
- ❖ Competition.
- ❖ The "Have and the Have-Not Syndrome"
- ❖ A host of other things that break down the "fly as hell" concept.

Think about how good it would feel to be in the company of people who really listen to you, takes you seriously, roots for you, has respect for the person you are and the decisions you make, and is willing to provide you with objective feedback. This would mean you don't have to pretend or placate to any audience. You can just BE! Company like this keeps you grounded and away from an altered state of reality. This, my friends, is your 'clique'!

My grandfather used to share with me a million nuggets to cultivate a good life whenever he saw me. My favorite and most memorable one was:

"If you're the only thing smokin' in your group, then your group ain't s**t."

Simply put, his logic was that everyone in the group needs to bring something special; otherwise, your group will be prone to toxic behaviors that will eventually tear apart the group, essentially feeding off one another's weaknesses. When we feed off the weaknesses of others, we transition into social villains who justify our bad behavior by setting ourselves up as victims. Playing the victim keeps us from owning and dealing with our own s**t.

Don't play the victim. It's Bitter Tea!

Today, social connections should be about what we have in common by way of life experiences and interests. Majoring in the minors of life involves all the nuances of how a person got to where they are, what they have, and how they obtained what they have. All these things cause us to rate ourselves (if you will) and nothing good can ever come from that! We are where we are and have what we have because that's the way it is! Of course, we can share our personal journey — and should — because that will help someone get prepared for their journey. This can be the beautiful thing about having a 'clique'. They are your personal "life concierge". They should be able to talk to you about the hard stuff. As well, they have to be willing to share with you on emotional and personal levels so that everyone will have the opportunity to be okay with who they are and where they have been.

Your clique needs to accept the differences as uniqueness and not us them as a point to criticize. Most importantly, your clique will need to want to listen to you, too. No one can be scared to hear what the other has to say. Each must be woman enough not to take anything personally and, instead, chalk it up as part of the 'being great' process.

Remove fear so we can hear.

Remove fear so we can see.

Remove fear so we can truly BE!

You see, today, people fear you when they know you see them for who they really are. Why is that? If you are authentic, you should be able to be authentic anywhere you go. If you choose to flee, then your ass AIN'T RIGHT…and that's the True Tea.

Residue

This is where residue enters. Residue is that questionable behavior or uneasiness you're left thinking about long after talking or engaging with someone you consider a friend or confidant. Whatever they are saying is causing you to doubt what you thought you knew about them. The residue is what lies beneath what they are saying. For example, let's say someone loaned you money but your loan shark is having a confidential conversation with you about how they really feel about another who owes them money. While you're listening, you slowly start feeling the dagger pierce deep under your breastbone. That's residue…and it can be found at the bottom of your teacup.

WHICH LEADS ME TO…

Taking Responsibility

There are those of us who make others responsible for our inability to take responsibility for our actions. Don't get mad when someone tells you about yourself because if you were managing "self" well, no one would have to tell you anything or compensate for the inappropriate behavior you choose to present to them. When engaging with others, it is very important to self-manage. This way, you are in control of what you say along with the behavior that may or may not support that behavior. On the off-chance you aren't in control of yourself during this particular engagement and another person chooses to spill your tea, you can't get mad because it's all about being able to train your dragon. If you can't (or don't), there will always be someone ready for an impromptu training session!

Self-Awareness

The point here is to be self-aware and, at the same time, open enough to receive feedback. It just might make you better! Feedback is often provided by people who are choosing to make an investment in your well-being. Commend that person's willingness to share the hard stuff with you. Thank him or her for sharing because it's a privilege for someone to choose YOU to share their personal feeling or experiences with. This is what that can sound like: "I appreciate you sharing this with me. I understand you really didn't have to." What the simplicity of that statement does is soften the intensity of what is being shared. You may not want to hear it, but that doesn't mean the person doesn't need to share. This is called "Creating a Safe Place of

Comfort"—a place for someone to pour their personal tea into your cup.

Now, no one said you have to just take anything. Be honest: If you don't want to hear it, then say, "This is not a conversation for me." There's no good reason to render anyone disabled just because they happened to be engaging in a conversation of which you don't want to be a part. Also, if you have a similar experience, share it with them. This is called "Building Trust" and, at the same time, you are making them comfortable. Never let someone give it all up to you before they have decided you are willing to make the investment in them.

If you are really paying attention, then you are perfectly aware of where a person is headed in conversation, so don't be lazy and let the chips fall where they may. Take accountability and simply say, "Hey, I'm not going to make the investment." This will definitely create a dialogue and make the person more selective about how they are choosing and what they are choosing to communicate…and to whom.

Personal Engagement

My point here is that if we are all more responsible in the way we choose to engage one another, then there should be no residue spilling over. Spilled residue is the stuff that leaves a person feeling icky about situations where things are constantly going unresolved. This causes people to be uncomfortable around one another or distant, behaving much like there is bad blood—where it is nothing more than an ill-handled engagement.

When I was a child, my grandmother used to tell me, "If you feel it first, then it's yours to tend to." As an adult, that simple statement helped me keep my engagements with others clear. Personal engagement can be very difficult because we can know people for years and never know that they are meeting us every day with their representative. The "representative" is the equivalent of the in-your-face 'Catfish' experience. This is when a person sees you and establishes where they are going to put you in their agenda, all while developing a persona fit to support the madness.

We have to address this and other behaviors truthfully, honestly, and with grace. Our society is all about telling it like it is and not letting anyone get the best of us. It's important to be mindful of how you throw your words at another person, especially when they are in a vulnerable state. Approach each situation with poise and decency. Think about what you want the person to leave with and who you want to be in each circumstance.

Straight Up From the Teacup

"A lack of boundaries invites a lack of respect."
~ Unknown ~

Encouragement

If the conversation is personal about you, proceed with caution and answer what is being asked (you can't be held responsible for them not knowing what questions to ask). If the conversation is general "listening", then respond without interjecting yourself (this is not meant for you to be narcissistic; it's not about you and your experiences). Once they have said their piece, leave them with empowerment. Leave that "Let me tell you what you should do" or "Let me tell you what I would do if it were me" at the door. End with a word of encouragement and slow sip of Raspberry Tea.

Love and Acceptance

I talk a lot about thinking of others before or while you are thinking of yourself. Body language is a great way to detect just how engaged others are in conversation. Paying attention to body language allows one to know when enough is enough, more is needed, or you're toast during conversation. No one will ever have to tell you when to stop if you pay attention to the signs.

Think about why someone chose YOU to talk to. Sometimes, people need an ear; not your opinion. Really marinate of that for a minute. Think about how many times you've heard someone say to you, "I just really needed a listening ear" or "I need someone to talk to". Well they are telling you what they need. If they seem a bit ungrateful about the advice or stories chosen to be shared, just think back to their initial request of your time.

We spend a lot of time insinuating ourselves in areas of the engagement that really aren't beneficial to the other person. They wind up having to tell you, "No, thank you" or straight-up, "This isn't about you." That may seem a bit rude, but if you listened to their request, no one will have to be insulted or feel dismissed.

After my failed marriage, I found myself wondering more often than not how to get consistent enjoyment out of every relationship. Is this possible? So, I decided to do research…starting with me. I asked myself a few simple questions:

- ❖ Do I consistently enjoy myself and why?
- ❖ Would someone else enjoy me, too?
- ❖ Where is my focus as it relates to connecting with another person?
- ❖ What am I willing to do after making the connection?
- ❖ How do we cultivate this connection?
- ❖ Lastly, how do I keep me, myself, and I out of the state of our relationship?

Toni Dupree

"For any relationship to be successful, the focus has to be on the giving and not the receiving."
~ Toni Dupree ~

A wonderful friend of mine once said, "For a marriage to be successful, there needs to be two givers joined in matrimony." That's when I came up with the quote above. Asking ourselves in-depth and personal questions helps rid us of that "taking ourselves too seriously" element. If the focus is taken off of one's self and put on the relationship, there will be no power struggles. One of my favorite quotes is from The Temptations movie:

"No one is bigger than the group!"

If we take this approach when dealing with our relationships—whether platonic or romantic—there will be no room for all of the insecurities, low self-esteem moments, power trips, and ridiculous behaviors that manifest all in the name of "love and acceptance".

Let's Cha-Cha Chat about our words matching our deeds!

A conversation should be conversational. Communication is very important in every relationship. We all know this, right? What we may not know is what you choose to discuss is just as important.

Let's use gossip as an example. No good comes from gossip because it's a toxic conversation. The only function of a toxin is to cause disease. Unfortunately, gossip will destroy both relationships: the person you are sharing the gossip with and the person you are gossiping about.

Be mindful of how and what you choose to communicate.

Think about the way a person answers the telephone. Is their ill tone of voice directed at you OR could they be going through something at that moment? My best advice is to take a moment to simply ask, "How's your day?" If the conversation starts out being all about you, catch yourself and apologize for making the conversation about you. At first engagement of a call or face-to-face encounter, listen and pay attention to social cues. If you are on the phone, listen to their breathing pattern. If face-to-face, look at the person's body language and pull back where there's a need and ease up when necessary. If you notice something has grown cold, it's not always the other person's fault. Sometimes, you may be the culprit.

Self-involved people are exasperating!

Believe me: Even if the words are never spoken, one's behavior will display a true irritation for the self-involved individual. If you have the luxury of being in someone's company, take note of their body language and eye contact. If you happen to be in mixed company, it may not be the time to ask questions. Still, take note and adjust your behavior accordingly.

Look: We all know what it feels like when we've rubbed another person the wrong way, said too much, said the wrong thing, insinuated ourselves where we shouldn't have, not given the proper amount of compassion, etc. The key is to think about how you want to feel, be addressed, and/or invited into a personal engagement. Then, take a moment to consider another person's feelings. Now, if you are unsure, pay attention to your surroundings. Ask your friends to help you navigate through this process…if they are close enough to you.

We have to get comfortable with productive feedback—the kind of information you can take in and give life to it. Most times, it's hard to receive feedback because you're not sure if you can trust the one who's giving it. Look at it like this: It's not so much about who's giving the feedback; it's more about what you choose to do with the feedback you're given. My grandmother often said, "Child, consider the source". My mother's rebuttal was, "Yeah, while that's true, you can even learn from a fool!"

We have this unnatural expectation of friends and loved ones. We expect a lot from others but expect very little of ourselves. What's crazy to me is being a person's friend, you always have to figure out what the "unnatural expectation" is, such as what your responses should be to them or about them when you are interacting with other people. It is much easier when you know what your idiosyncrasies are and be able to share them with others so that they aren't left feeling as if they are a scorned child when that misstep happens. It's about consideration. If consideration is taken…well, into consideration all the time, then we aren't left with having to maneuver through life like we are working a crossword puzzle!

I've asked myself why this is far too many times to count. So, after conducting a series of interviews, I'm left to believe we hold others to a higher standard because it takes the burden of "accountability" off of us! For example, something happens on your end and you choose not to address it in that moment but opted, instead, to wait days later. First of all, the other person may have already dealt with it or decided not to point the finger, all the while hoping that you would take responsibility and simply say, "I apologize for any confusion." What that does is let them know you are accountable and will take responsibility. I find that a little change in perspective modified the outcome of the situation on a broader scale—but for the better of the relationship. With that being said, instead of putting undo expectations on others, how about bringing a little accountability to our own lives?

Here are some examples:

- ❖ Be responsible and accountable for yourself first.
- ❖ Take no prisoners.
- ❖ Understand that most of our outcomes are contingent on our own behavior—the good, the bad, AND the ugly.

I find that our behavior can be our biggest obstacle, which leads me to trust my theory that our behavior is a true indication of how we value ourselves and others. Let's take, for example, the procrastinator. Do they drag their asses because they feel unworthy to go the extra mile for themselves? What about the person with the bad attitude who is really putting on a show in a loud, rude, and obnoxious manner in public? Is he or she manifesting behavior that is in line with how they view themselves? Could that be the reason there is never any sign of embarrassment displayed when that type of behavior is presented in a public forum? Use those questions as ones to ponder over while reading the next paragraph…

Now comes the big question: Does our environment dictate our behavior? I believe that sometimes it can but that isn't the real issue. The REAL issue is us allowing the environment or other people to dictate our behavior. If an individual grew up poor (for example), is that the catalyst that permits them to behave badly? No. It's a crutch — and we should be able to identify the difference. It's important to know who you are and be honest about that knowledge. Know what you are willing to do and why. Take the risks associated with that knowing and have the strength to live and tell your story. All of these attributes are components of confidence.

Make a point to take an inventory of your life right now and be honest with yourself. Ask yourself: Is this the best place for me to be? Why or why not? Is your life based on what others think about you? If so, why? If the answers to those questions are not acceptable to you, then do things differently.

If there are things about you that you don't like, you can best believe no one else will like those things, either. However, use caution here: Don't change because of others. Change because it's necessary for YOU! Changing because of someone else breaks down your confidence and if you do all of that 'changing' and they still don't want you, now what? You've found yourself in a worse place—not because of them but because of YOU.

Have you ever heard the phrase, "Your attitude determines your altitude"? This phrase means your approach determines how far you will go in your life. For example, if you only see yourself the way others see you, then you can only go as far as their view can take you and that, my friends, is very sad.

My late stepfather, Ronald Taylor, instilled the following saying in me:

"Be the person you aspire to be long before you meet your mate!"

Never let the people around you dictate how far you will go in life. Prayerfully, you have already started becoming a person with confidence and your sharing is just that: sharing. You aren't seeking permission or acceptance from others. Have you ever started to tell someone something that you are doing and their response was, "Yeah. I think you should do that"? Meanwhile, you're thinking, "I wasn't asking for your approval!"

Speaking life into a situation involves a lot of listening and commending a person's zest or courage. I want to believe that most of us mean well and plan to give well in conversation but come up short during the articulation phase. This is when you would be wonderful by letting it go because you understand their intent, even if it was or wasn't intentional because that's not the point. Responding to minor behaviors you don't agree with can throw you off your major moment. So, be grand and "let them have that". Move forward. If it happens again, then you know you can't share things of major proportions with them anymore.

    I used to belly-ache about why people said certain things to me or replied in a lackluster manner. It took me a long time to realize that's not what I'm supposed to be trying to figure out. I grew up in a household with a mother who "told it like it was". As challenging as her delivery may have been, I always appreciated the candor. My mom had many tough-talk scripts that she shared with me that kept me on my toes. One that immediately comes to mind is, "Don't ever work so hard to be what others like; work harder at your development." I was like, "What???" LOL! My mom has always talked to me like I was older. Her reasoning was that she talked to me where I was going and into whom I was supposed to be. I often wonder why we choose not to talk to one another for where we are going. I have this thing about what I allow people to pour into me. Tell me the truth as it is; not as you see it.

Now, **THAT'S** the real tea!

Straight Up From the Teacup

Down to Business:
No Black and White.
Just Shades of Grey!

I have always wanted to write about best business practices. Having such a vast customer service background—laced with an amazing amount of retail experience—I feel very confident in sharing my "Earl Grey Tea Style" of doing business. The Earl Grey Tea Style of business is about being "Poised, Professional, and Prepared."

Poised:
Keeping your composure makes your client feel that you are more than capable of managing the situation.

Professional:
Lets your client know that you will not administer petty or common behavior while doing business.

Prepared:
This makes your client secure in that you know what you are doing and they can trust that you will do it.

Now, with that being said, I don't feel the customer is always right. When a person feels disappointed about the way they have been treated isn't about being wrong or right. When we get into placing blame, we lose sight of fixing the problem. There is a reason why it's said that we need to know right from wrong: It's the first step to taking responsibility for our actions. If we start from the place where everyone in every situation and every time gets the same respect and consideration—no matter the outcome of the transaction—no one will leave feeling mistreated or disrespected.

Being an entrepreneur—being a "Boss" in business for yourself or running someone else's business—is hard, to say the least! Ha! You have to deal with many, many, MANY interesting personalities…but that's not the hard part. The hard part is offering civilized service, no matter what type of client you happen to encounter. So, one issue as a business owner or "Boss" is that in your head, you have a lot of preconceived information about your clients (potential or otherwise). Another issue is you believe what's in your head, which means you have created a built-in bias. I have a name for that: Professional Suicide. I say this because what you feel about your clients is exactly how you will treat them. A great remedy is to treat everyone better than they are behaving.

For example, if I have an irate client who is displeased about something associated with the services I provide or a product I am selling, I need to listen to the client's displeasure and then ask, "What would you like to happen in an effort to correct or make good on this unfortunate situation?" After they share what they want, you should already be thinking about what you are willing to do while they were talking. As a boss, you are equipped to do more than one thing at a time, right? Next, apologize and leave the issue alone. It's now time to resolve it. This is not a debate. The point is not to win over the client. The point is to fix the issue. Even if they choose to never do business with you again, what they know about you is that you are Poised, Professional, and Prepared! In business terms, you are full of integrity.

Now, let's bring it home.

Do what is right for your business with your client in mind—and feel good about your choice. You see, at this point, you have listened, considered them as part of exploring options to rectify the issue, and taken responsibility. Now, you have to go big or they go home. They key is not to give the client what they want for 'business sake' because all business owners understand that we have to be willing to lose in order to gain. They key is to simply make the best decision for your business by keeping your client in mind.

"Leaving any engagement on a high note maximizes our momentum to land the next more successful one."
~ **Toni Dupree** ~

Salty? I Ain't Salty!

When I think about Salted Caramel, it brings me to that deep-down bitterness that causes a 'salty' reaction brought on by a simple trigger. This behavior manifests due to the residue left over from all the negativity that has been poured into you, leaving you acting 'salty' and unsavory.

This causes feelings of inadequacy, which triggers bad understandings, defensiveness, and lashing out during social interactions that sometimes becomes more of a personal nature. For example, if you are single, nearing 40, have no children but want them; then, someone who does not know that your not having children is a sore spot asks, "Why don't you have children?" At that point, you lose it!

In my previous marriage, there were things that simply weren't right. Of course, I tried to mention what I was feeling. Unfortunately, I had tolerated those "wrongs" for far too long. So, when I decided to talk, my delivery was less than desirable. The residue had already set in by the time I decided to discuss the issues.

Today, before deciding to talk to anyone about anything, I make it a point to ask myself some questions:

Am I committed to making this investment? This means that I have to be just fine with doing my part.

Will what I'm considering discussing with them matter tomorrow, the next day, or even three months from now?

I Said I am NOT Salty!

A classic example of not allowing someone to pull you into their saltiness follows. This is an actual text message received during the publication of this book. My direct response to the message follows immediately after:

"Good morning, Toni. I normally keep it classy and it is what it is, but after several weeks of praying and stirring, I felt that I must address the issue at hand because it was very hurtful to me. I have gone through so much, but what don't kill me will only make me stronger. I am an adult and certainly not a messy individual. You do not have to respond back at this point but I must get off my chest. When I met you, I really thought God was placing a genuine friend that would help me with what I was going through and we become very close friends. But I guess like my grandmother taught me: An individual that will speak ill of her so-called friends that you constantly stated you were letting go of but was constantly in their presence, then I should have known you were not genuine with me. My friendship meant absolutely nothing. I thought it was somewhat strange that you would try and take over a friendship that you met

through me and supposedly had issues from the very beginning with her but continued to gravitate towards a close friendship. I would have never tried to become close to someone that was your friend without you being present. I was so shocked and hurt when it was revealed to me how I was constantly a topic of your negative conversation. We are all adults and if you had an issue with me, I certainly thought with all your etiquette training you would have been woman enough to come to me with any issues you had with me. Sometimes, God places people there alongside of you to warn you and to help prevent the hurt and pain. As a matter-of-fact, I was advised it's not worth addressing this issue with you but I am the type that must get it off my chest and then I can continue on. This is why I have never fooled with a lot of women because I can't stand petty gossip. You be blessed and an individual of your caliber (etiquette coach), I really don't need an explanation. God is good to me. I just need to allow that discerning spirit to take over in my life. I wish you well."

My Response:

"I wish you well as well."

Sometimes, we talk about things we don't care about just to get a reaction from another person. What's really going on is that we aren't getting what we need from the relationship and are allowing our lack to cause us to misbehave in an unsavory manner.

Lastly, I won't allow too much time to pass before having the conversation. It's perfectly fine to wait a decent amount of time to organize your thoughts and gain perspective. However, waiting so long that the other person has to ask, "What the hell are you talking about?" is TOO long.

Unfortunately, that is our society. We speak randomly about things and, most often, mean no harm. That does not take away the 'saltiness' of the situation, however. It's healthy to allow yourself to feel an emotion such as anger, but it's counterproductive to get stuck in that emotion and use it as an excuse to act out. This has nothing to do with being the "bigger person"; it's about not allowing yourself to "happen" to your situations.

Toni Dupree

Cleaning Up Our Act

Straight Up From the Teacup

We typically start thinking about detoxing when we have consumed too much of something in our diet that goes against our healthy eating regimen. I see nothing wrong with applying this same concept in our social engagements.

Implement clean conversation regimen by managing how you talk to others and what you talk to them about. For example, if I'm only talking about dismay and mess, the return on that isn't going to be great. See, you get as good as you give. If all you are giving is the bottom of the barrel, then you can be sure to get only that in return.

At times, it may appear like we are not taking a journey together. You may not be walking my walk at the same time, but you will likely be traveling down the same road. This means we are fit to be a guide for one another — if the decision is made to do so. I've learned that detoxing doesn't mean throwing someone or something away. Rather, it's a matter of repositioning (if you will).

When I was younger, I was so very "final". The interesting thing about finality is that it's forever. You never get the chance to learn, grow, and develop from whatever situation got the best of you because any opportunity for rectification was destroyed. Unfortunately, there are those situations that are best destroyed because no good can come from them; however, a lesson is always there to be learned. I believe the toxins have to be destroyed but that everything else can be saved if all parties are willing to work at it. This is why I believe it is better to always take a personal inventory of what you are allowing in, what you are letting go, and why. When detoxing, it's VERY important to know the "Whys?" of it all.

Straight Up From the Teacup

    See, you have to able to know WHY any breakdown occurred and WHY you are choosing to salvage (or WHY not). How do you stop it from reoccurring? These "Whys?" are important for you because when faced with a conversation to explain yourself, there will be no residue that leads to guilt that will cause you to continue — all the while knowing: THIS JUST AIN'T RIGHT! The other thing to consider is: Who wants to live a life guilty with overdue residue?

Toni Dupree

Refine your conversation with a polished delivery.

Straight Up From the Teacup

The tea bag was created by Thomas Sullivan by accident in 1908. He was a tea purveyor, and to increase tea sales, he put samples of different teas in little silk bags. Before long, his customers were requesting his tea bags.

Much like gossip or storytelling, the way a story is told or delivered causes listeners to want more or be turned completely off. Perhaps you go through a bad break-up but somehow managed to find your "girl-power". People will be all "peoply" and want to hear the nitty-gritty of the break-up but will grow uninterested in the fact that you have gotten your power and become more assertive due to being able to let the toxic parts go. You will have to be very careful to tell your story in a way that doesn't step on another's toes. It's not about biting your tongue; it's about knowing how much of your story to share. Sharing your story should give life, not take it.

For example, you just landed a huge client but a co-worker is still learning the ropes when you share your good news. Your evident joy shouldn't make him or her want to resign. Remember: Sometimes, less is more.

Straight Up From the Teacup

"I love living and am committed to doing it in a great, big, wonderful way. Hopefully, you'll join me because I can't do it all by myself."
~ Toni Dupree ~

Toni Dupree

A still, flavorful build.

Straight Up From the Teacup

My editor asked me what it is I wanted to leave with my readers. Honestly, there isn't just ONE thing. This book is all-encompassing. When we involve ourselves in other people's lives, it's natural to not first consider what valuable nuggets we have to share with them that will enrich their lives. I believe if we start thinking upfront about how we plant to show up for each other, it would be a bit easier to figure out our relationships.

Straight Up from the Teacup is about taking a closer look inside ourselves and getting down to the "Tea of the Matter", so to speak. You know how sometimes we ask ourselves, "Why am I having to deal with so much "peoply" stuff?"? It's always an issue or two with someone about something that really doesn't matter, but you're still having to deal with it. UGH! Then, you start going back reflecting on other relationships and say to yourself, "What's different about them?" Then, you take a closer look at your inner circle, your "Know You Crew", 'clique', buds (almost Colombo-like)…ya got me? We're not looking for a scapegoat but more of a reason to gain understanding in order to gain perspective.

Answer these couple of questions: In the relationships where you're having to constantly talk about nonsense, do all parties involved have room to be who they truly are? Are you forcing someone to interact as their representative?

See, we sometimes will to us what we create in us. Okay. Walk with me here…

When you spend a lot of time making nothing look like something because you don't want to be found out, you create a representative (a better version of who you really are, instead of doing the work to just be a better YOU). We sometimes give too much of what people don't need, which is proven evident by the way they respond to what is poured into them.

I wrote this book to assist in making our social engagements less complicated and dysfunctional by sharing some tools to eliminate the residue and reduce the amount of "peoply" stuff we have to engage in.

"What do we live for, if not to make life less difficult for each other?"
~ George Eliot ~

That is my favorite quote. It reminds me of why God put us all here together. If I'm thinking of you, my question should never be, "Who's thinking of me?" When you are having to tackle something big and stressful, think about it in relation to tea. Handle it like a nice, slow steep and finish it with a light sip.

… Toni Dupree

Talk About Your Teas

In this section, write about your personal reflections on communication styles using your personal favorite types of tea. Be inspired to "taste" your words used during daily interactions and how they impact your discussions with others platonically, romantically, and professionally.

Straight Up From the Teacup

Toni Dupree

Straight Up From the Teacup

Toni Dupree

Straight Up From the Teacup

Toni Dupree

Straight Up From the Teacup

Toni Dupree

ABOUT THE AUTHOR

Toni Dupree

*Best-Selling Author and
President of Etiquette & Style by Dupree*

Straight Up From the Teacup

Toni Dupree is Founder and President of *Etiquette & Style by Dupree* (ESD), an etiquette training and coaching company based in Houston, Texas with a mission to help young people and business professionals get ahead with good manners. Since 2006, her etiquette workshops, style seminars, and self-esteem and behavior classes have taught hundreds of individuals—from youth groups to business gatherings—how to present their best selves and cultivate meaningful, productive relationships.

A Houston native, Toni was introduced to the social graces as a child when she attended Mildred Johnson's Charm and Etiquette Academy. Her training there helped prepare her for work as a model, pageant participant, speaker, and facilitator. She is a graduate of the Interior Arts School of Design in Houston, Texas and Jack Yates High School. Toni has also earned certification from the Center for Organizational Cultural Competence in Winnipeg, Canada and completed coursework in Psychology and Behavioral Analysis from Kaplan University.

Prior to launching ESD, Toni volunteered as a Youth Mentor at Houston's Trinity United Methodist Church, organizing self-esteem workshops, fashion show preparation sessions, and etiquette classes for young people. While working as a Trainer at the Houston Area Women's Center, she developed business etiquette workshops and taught life skills classes for the organization's clients, laying the foundation for the creation of ESD in 2006.

In addition to offering customized etiquette workshops, business environment training, and life skills coaching sessions to young adults and business professionals in Houston and beyond, Toni writes an etiquette column for

MVMNT Magazine called *An Etiquette Perspective*. She also published her first book in 2015, *Whose Fork is it Anyway?* — an entertaining and easy-to-read dining guide for young adults. In 2018, she participated in an anthology, *There Is Life After...*, which became an Amazon Best-Selling title.

Toni lives in the Houston area where she volunteers with the Fort Bend Education Foundation Auxiliary — a nonprofit creating community awareness; Makeover 101 — a nonprofit ministry; Village of Winkler — an elderly community; and Houston Can Academy — a second-chance high school for teens considering dropping out of high school.

Connect With Toni Dupree

- ❖ Web: ingoodcompanyetiquette.com/houston
- ❖ Email: chytonya.dupree@yahoo.com
- ❖ Facebook: cdupree1471 (personal)
- ❖ Facebook: DupreeAcademy (business)
- ❖ Instagram: @EtiquetteAndStyle
- ❖ Twitter: @iam_etiquette
- ❖ LinkedIn: @Toni-Dupree-b984b015
- ❖ Phone: 832.407.3117

Other Publications By & With Toni Dupree

Available for purchase on Amazon at:

www.amazon.com/Whose-Fork-Anyway-Toni-Dupree/dp/1515311112

Available for purchase on Amazon at:

www.amazon.com/There-Life-After-Linda-Williams/dp/0991537718

Toni's Quotes
"Tell It Like It Is Teas!"

"You can't romance the devil and then wonder why you're left with nothing."
~ Toni Dupree ~

*"So, you want to be loved?
Then be everything you
want in another...
but more."*
~ **Toni Dupree** ~

Straight Up From the Teacup

"Embrace your inner lady-like naughtiness while you wait to see "Fifty Shades of Grey".
~ **Toni Dupree** ~

"Inspire by creating magic in the most ordinary place."
~ **Toni Dupree** ~

"Customer service isn't dead. The acceptance of bad behaviors forfeits the chance for great service ahead. But, like any major trend, it takes the best designer to bring it back again."
~ **Toni Dupree** ~

"Being transparent isn't about losing your freedom of privacy. It's about freely sharing on your terms in an effort to bring comfort to someone else."
~ Toni Dupree ~

"Life is truly about creating the most beautiful experiences for someone else."
~ **Toni Dupree** ~

"My true love, I love you forever, always, and just because…"
~ Toni Dupree ~

Straight Up From the Teacup

"My mama taught me how to love naked and deeply."
~ Toni Dupree ~

"This unspeakable love that ain't so neat. Passion fiery and sweet with a slow burn that goes straight to the white meat."
~ Toni Dupree ~

www.ingramcontent.com/pod-product-compliance
Lightning Source LLC
Chambersburg PA
CBHW071530080526
44588CB00011B/1622